A TO Z CAREERS IN HEALTH AND SOCIAL CARE IN THE UNITED KINGDOM:

A HANDBOOK FOR STUDENTS AND CROSS PROFESSIONALS

CRISFORD CHOGUGUDZA

Copyright © 2025 CRISFORD CHOGUGUDZA

No part of this book may be reproduced, distributed, or transmitted in any form or by any means, including photocopying, recording, or other electronic or mechanical methods, without the prior written permission of the publisher and the author, except in the case of brief quotations used in reviews or certain other noncommercial uses permitted by copyright law.

Publisher: Upway Books
Author: CRISFORD CHOGUGUDZA
Title: A to Z Careers in Health and Social Care in the United Kingdom,
A Handbook for Students and Cross Professionals
ISBN: 978-1-917916-65-3
Cover Designed on Canva: www.canva.com

This book is a work of non-fiction. The information it contains is based on the author's research, experience, and knowledge at the time of publication. The publisher and authors have made every effort to ensure the accuracy and reliability of the information provided, but assume no responsibility for any errors, omissions, or differing interpretations of the subject matter. This publication is not intended to replace professional advice or consultation. Readers are encouraged to seek professional guidance where appropriate.

contact@upwaybooks.com
www.upwaybooks.com

CONTENTS

Preface 5

Chapter 1 7

Chapter 2 11

Chapter 3 37

Chapter 4: 39

Chapter 5: 41

Chapter 6 43

Conclusion 43

References 44

PREFACE

Living abroad especially in England for more than 20 years, where I gained a profound academic and professional interest in health and social care has given me the motivation to focus particularly in this area for book project, which is rapidly gaining currency in UK at large. This handbook outlines the nature of the health and social care profession in UK and why many people choose health and social care for a career. The handbook provides a detailed list of health and social care careers in the UK. I wish to thank my friends, family and colleagues for there moral support. I could not have achieved this milestone without my family (*Sister Miriam, my children Mya, Khwezi, Macky and Kelvin among special others*), colleagues and well-wishers. They pushed me to finally realise this goal of publishing my book idea which started abstractly a decade ago. This handbook is my gift to the wider health and social care industry which contributed immensely to my academic and professional development. It is also an area that has given sanctuary and professional comfort to thousands of immigrants previously marginalised in other professional areas due to a variety of reasons.

CHAPTER 1
WHAT IS HEALTH AND SOCIAL CARE

Health and Social Care (often abbreviated to *HSC* or *H&SC*) is a term that relates to services that are available from health and social care providers in the UK and indeed in US, Australia, Canada, New Zealand and Ireland. This is a generic term which refers to the whole of the healthcare provision infrastructure, and private sector. As a discipline or area of study, Health and Social Care (H&SC) combines elements of sociology, biology, nutrition, law, and ethics. Typically, students of Health and Social Care may take a health and social care course as a route to further qualifications such as social work, nursing or public health hoping that to get better employment opportunities in the wider sector. Depending on their qualification level, some students may start off as health care assistant, care workers etc. and develop care pathways to become doctors, nurses, social workers, physiotherapists, counsellors, psychotherapists, paramedics, or other related kindred professions. In the UK in particular, Health and Social Care courses can be studied in schools and colleges from Key Stage 4/GCSE Level (age 14–16), colleges and for adults over 18 years in some universities and community colleges across the United Kingdom. Level 3 is the foundation level which offers a certificate and can be accessed by people with lower academic qualifications. One can exit at Foundation Stage or proceed to the Diploma, Degree and Masters from Level 4 to

Level 7. This course attracts a lot of candidates from wider sections of society including those already working in the Care Industry. There is a high level of optimism amongst the students studying health and social care hence the increasing interest in the course in the United Kingdom.

Why Choose Health and Social Care Careers in UK

Choosing a course to study has always been a challenge for many students both young and old. Studying health and social care in the England in particular, offers a rewarding career trajectory, access to a high standard of education, and the chance to make a significant impact on vulnerable people, the underserved and those seeking a passionate career choice. Over 2 million people across England work in health and social care and related roles. There are opportunities across the entire health and social care which attract a significant number of prospective students want to join this growing profession. It is expected that if one wants to study health and social care, they need to familiarise with the benefits of studying the course. Health and social care is one profession among a few where there is a significant number of students from a widening participation spectrum, where everyone is welcome regardless of qualifications. The area of health and social care has also attracted hundreds of candidates from immigrant communities who were recruited from abroad through the Certificate of Sponsorship (COS). This is a course which is easy to join in which students can easily transfer their skills (communication and problem solving) and assimilate with little or no difficulties at all. Some join health and social care as a calling, some see it as a rewarding career while others find opportunities to Specialise in related areas such as mental health gerontology among others.

WHAT DOES A HEALTH AND SOCIAL CARE WORKER ACTUALLY DO?

The day-to-day reality of what health and social care is comes alive through its workforce. The sector offers an incredibly diverse range of roles, each playing a vital part in supporting individuals' wellbeing. Whether you're drawn to direct clinical care, hands-on support, or essential back-office functions, there's a place for your skills. To truly understand what health and social care workers do, it's important to look beyond job titles and see how these professionals apply core values, such as dignity, empathy, and safeguarding, in real-world settings across London. From assisting with personal care and medication to developing individualised care plans and supporting community integration, their work is rooted in person-centred practice.

"A modern health and social care system has to be completely focused on the needs of its users."

— Patricia Hewitt

CHAPTER 2

The list below covers a wide range of roles, from frontline clinical positions to support, technical, and administrative careers, reflecting the diverse and interconnected nature of the sector.

A

Acupuncturist

Acupuncturists insert needles into pressure points on clients' bodies to help with stress and improve their wellbeing

Advanced Practitioner (Social Work)

Advanced Practitioners are highly experienced social workers who specialize in a particular area of practice, such as safeguarding or mental health. They often lead on complex cases and provide expert guidance to other social workers.

Advocacy Worker

Advocacy workers help give people a voice in decisions about their health or social care.

Anatomical Pathology Technician

Anatomical pathology technicians (APTs) help pathologists exam a body to work out the cause of death.

Advanced Clinical Practitioner (ACP):

These are experienced nurses, paramedics, pharmacists, or allied health professionals who undertake advanced Master's-level training to diagnose, treat, and manage complex patient care with a high degree of autonomy. They are a cornerstone of multi-disciplinary teams.

AI & Machine Learning Specialist in Healthcare:

They develop and implement AI algorithms to read medical images (e.g., detecting cancers on scans), predict patient deterioration, automate administrative tasks, and discover new drugs.

Adult Nurse: Provides care to adult patients who are injured, ill, or suffering from chronic physical or mental health conditions. They work in hospitals, communities, and homes.

Ambulance Care Assistant/Patient Transport Service (PTS) Driver: Transports patients to and from hospital appointments who are not in an emergency situation.

Approved Mental Health Professional (AMHP)

An AMHP is approved to carry out functions under the Mental Health Act 1983, and as such, they carry with them a warrant card, like police officers. The role of the AMHP is to coordinate the assessment of individuals who are being considered for detention under the Mental Health Act 1983.

Art Therapist/Art Psychotherapist:

Uses art as a form of psychotherapy to help clients express and understand their emotions and address psychological issues.

Audiologist:

Assesses, diagnoses, and manages hearing and balance disorders in patients of all ages.

B

Biomedical Scientist: Works in laboratory settings to perform tests on tissue and fluid samples to help diagnose disease and monitor treatments. They are crucial in pathology departments.

Breastfeeding Counsellor: Provides support, information, and encouragement to mothers and families about breastfeeding.

C

Care Assistant/Support Worker: Provides practical help and support to people with daily living, such as washing, dressing, eating, and social activities. They work in care homes, hospices, or people's own homes.

Care Coordinator / Personalised Care Specialist:

Work with patients with complex long-term conditions to navigate the health and social care system, ensuring they receive coordinated and personalised care plans. They act as a single point of contact.

Care Home Manager: Manages the daily operations of a residential or nursing care home, ensuring high-quality care and compliance with regulations (CQC).

Care Coordinator

Care Coordinators play a key role in organizing and managing care for individuals, particularly in healthcare or adult social care settings. They ensure that all aspects of a client's care are coordinated effectively, often working with multidisciplinary teams.

Care Worker

Care workers support vulnerable people with their daily activities and help them to live as independently as possible.

Children's Nurse

Children's nurses provide care for children and young people with health problems.

Child Protection Officer

Child protection officers promote children's wellbeing and protect them from harm or abuse.

Chiropractor

Chiropractors manipulate joints, bones and soft tissue to help clients control pain or prevent injuries from re-occurring.

Clinical Engineer

Clinical engineers design, develop and maintain medical equipment used to diagnose illness and treat patients.

Clinical Psychologist

Clinical psychologists help people manage mental health issues, phobias and addiction.

Clinical Bioinformatics Specialist:

Specifically work with genomic data. They develop and use software to analyse DNA sequences from patients, which is vital for personalised medicine, cancer treatment, and diagnosing rare genetic diseases. This field is booming thanks to the NHS Genomic Medicine Service.

Clinical Flow Coordinator:

Work in hospitals to optimise patient movement from admission to discharge. They use real-time data to manage bed capacity, reduce A&E waiting times, and prevent bottlenecks, ensuring patients get the right care in the right place at the right time.

Clinical Psychologist: Assesses and treats people with mental and physical health problems that are causing psychological distress, using psychological therapies.

Clinical Scientist

Clinical scientists research and develop techniques and equipment to help prevent, diagnose and treat illness.

Cognitive Behavioural Therapist (CBT)

Cognitive behavioural therapists help patients change negative patterns of thinking or behaviour with talking therapy.

Community Development Worker

Helps communities bring about change and improve the quality of life in their area.

Community Psychiatric Nurse (CPN)

Mental health nurse who works in the community, supporting patients with mental health conditions outside of hospital settings.

Counsellor

Provides a confidential talking therapy to help people explore their feelings, problems, and behaviours to facilitate positive change.

Critical Care Technologist

Critical care technologists monitor life support and other equipment used with critically ill patients.

D

Dental Nurse: Assists the dentist with all aspects of patient care, from preparing equipment to reassuring patients.

Dental Hygienist: Focuses on preventive dental health, treating gum disease and showing people how to maintain good oral health.

Dental Therapist: Can carry out routine dental procedures such as fillings and extractions on children and adults.

Digital Mental Health Practitioner:

They provide therapy and support through online platforms, video calls, and digital messaging services. They are experts in delivering effective mental health care remotely, making it more accessible.

Digital Health Specialist / mHealth Developer:

Develop, and evaluate digital health tools like health apps, wearable device integrations, telehealth platforms, and AI-powered diagnostic assistants. They ensure these technologies are clinically safe and effective.

Dietitian

Assesses, diagnoses, and treats dietary and nutritional problems using evidence-based research. They often work with patients who have specific medical conditions.

Dispensing Optician
Dispensing opticians give advice on vision care, and supply glasses and contact lenses to suit their customer's needs.

District Nurse
District nurses care for people outside of hospital in patients' homes, GP surgeries and residential care homes.

E

Emergency Care Assistant

Works alongside paramedics, driving emergency vehicles and assisting in providing immediate care to patients.

EMT (Emergency Medical Technician)

Provides emergency medical care and transport for patients. A role often found within ambulance services.

End of Life Care Worker/EOLC

A specialist care role focused on providing physical, emotional, and spiritual support to individuals and their families in the final stages of life.

Epidemiologist

Investigates patterns and causes of diseases in populations

F

Family Court Advisor FCA (Children's Guardian):

Provides essential support and guidance in family court proceedings, focusing on the welfare of children and ensuring their voices are heard.

Family Therapist

Helps people utilize the strengths of their relationships to overcome mental health problems.

Family Support Worker

Works with families facing difficult challenges, providing practical help and emotional support to keep families together and children safe.

Forensic Psychologist

Applies psychological theory to the understanding and prevention of criminal behaviour, often working in prisons, secure hospitals, or rehabilitation services.

G

General Practitioner (GP)

A doctor who is the first point of contact for patients in the community. They diagnose and treat a wide range of health conditions and refer patients to hospital specialists when needed.

Geneticist

Geneticists study how genes work in humans, animals, plants and microbes, and how they are passed on.

Genomic Counsellor:

Work with patients and families to explain complex genetic test results, what they mean for their health, and the potential implications for other family members. They provide crucial emotional and decision-making support.

H

Health Data Scientist / Health Informatician:

Analyse vast amounts of patient data (clinical, genetic, lifestyle) to identify trends, predict outbreaks, improve treatment protocols, and inform health policy. They are crucial for the NHS's move towards a more data-driven organisation.

Health Play Specialist

Uses play to help children in healthcare settings understand
and cope with their treatment and hospital experience.

Health Improvement Specialist

Develop and implement strategies to improve health in specific areas (e.g. physical activity, men)

Health Visitor

A qualified nurse or midwife with additional training who supports families with young children (typically 0-5 years) on issues like growth, development, and parenting.

Healthcare Assistant (HCA)

Supports nurses and other healthcare professionals with day-to-day patient care in hospitals, GP surgeries, and community settings.

Hospital Porter

Transports patients, medical equipment, and supplies around the hospital. A vital logistical role in the NHS.

Health Promotion Specialist

Health promotion specialists educate and inform people about health issues.

Homeopath

Homeopaths use homeopathic remedies to stimulate the body to heal itself.

Housing Officer/Manager

Housing officer/housing manager, is a professional who supports tenants in housing associations and local authority properties.

Hospice Worker

Provides palliative and end-of-life care in a hospice setting. The team includes nurses, doctors, counsellors, and support staff.

Hypnotherapist

Hypnotherapists use hypnosis to help people make positive changes to their health, lifestyle and behaviours.

I

Interpreter (Health)

Provides language translation services to ensure non-English speaking patients can communicate effectively with healthcare staff and understand their treatment.

K

Key Worker (in Learning Disabilities/Social Care)

Provides consistent, one-to-one support to an individual with learning disabilities, helping them to live independently and access community activities.

L

Learning Disability Nurse

Specialises in supporting people with learning disabilities to live independent and fulfilling lives, promoting their health and wellbeing.

LGBTQ+ Support Worker

Provides targeted support and advocacy for LGBTQ+ individuals within health and social care services.

M

Maternity Support Worker

Maternity support workers help midwives care for women and their babies before, during and after childbirth.

Medical Herbalist

Medical herbalists use plants and herbal remedies to help improve their clients' health and wellbeing.

Medical Illustrator

Medical illustrators produce photographs, videos and graphical images for use in healthcare treatment and training.

Medical Physicist

Medical physicists design, develop and test the scanning and imaging equipment used in the diagnosis and treatment of patients.

Mental Health Nurse: Works with patients who have mental health conditions, providing therapy, medication management, and support in hospitals or the community.

Microbiologist

Microbiologists study organisms like bacteria, viruses, fungi and algae to make advances in environmental science, medicine and agriculture.

Midwife

Provides care and support to women and their families during pregnancy, labour, and the postnatal period.

Music Therapist

Uses music to help people of all ages improve their emotional wellbeing, address psychological issues, and support rehabilitation.

N

Naturopath

Naturopaths believe in improving their clients' health through natural therapies and education about lifestyle, diet and exercise.

Neonatal Nurse

Cares for newborn babies who are born prematurely or who are sick, working in specialist neonatal units (SCBU/NICU).

Neurophysiotherapist

A physiotherapist who Specialises in treating people with conditions affecting the brain and nervous system, such as stroke or Parkinson's disease.

Newly Qualified Social Workers (NQSWs)

Newly qualified social workers are those who have recently completed their degree in social work and are starting their careers. In the UK, NQSWs typically undergo an Assessed and Supported Year in Employment (ASYE) to transition from academic learning to professional practice.

Nurse

Nurses care for adults who are sick, injured or have physical disabilities and are mostly based in hospitals. Nursing Homes and other health institutions.

Becoming a Nurse: https://www.healthcareers.nhs.uk/explore-roles/nursing/how-become-nurse

Nursing Associate

Nursing associates care for sick people of all ages in hospital and in the community, working closely with registered nurses.

Neonatal Nurse

Care for newborn babies who are born premature or sick and may have problems such as respiratory difficulties or nutritional needs.

Nutritional Therapist

Nutritional therapists help people by giving advice on diet, nutrition and lifestyle.

O

Occupational Health Nurse

Occupational health nurses care for the health and wellbeing of people at work.

Occupational Therapist (OT)

Helps people of all ages to overcome challenges in doing everyday activities (occupations) due to illness, disability, or accident.

Oncology Nurse

Specialise in caring for cancer patients providing treatment and support during their battle with disease

Operating Department Practitioner (ODP)

A specialist role working in operating theatres, supporting patients before, during, and after surgery (anesthetic, surgical, and recovery roles).

Ophthalmologist

Medical doctors are medical doctors specializing in eye care, capable of diagnosing and treating a wide range of eye conditions, performing surgeries, and prescribing corrective lenses.

Optometrist

Examines eyes, diagnoses sight problems, and can prescribe glasses or contact lenses. They can also detect signs of eye disease and other health conditions.

Optometry Nurse,

Often referred to as an ophthalmic nurse, specializes in providing care related to eye health and vision, assisting in the diagnosis and treatment of various eye conditions

P

Paediatricians

Paediatricians diagnose and treat health conditions that affect babies, children and young people.

Pediatric Nurse

Pediatric nurses are healthcare professionals who provide specialized care to children at various stages of development.

Paramedic

Provides immediate emergency medical care to people in crisis situations, often as the first senior healthcare professional on the scene.

Pharmacist

Experts in medicines who work in community pharmacies (high street chemists), hospitals, or GP practices to ensure the safe and effective use of medication.

Pharmacy assistant

Pharmacy assistants serve customers and patients in chemists and hospital dispensaries.

Pharmacy Technician

Supports pharmacists in preparing and dispensing prescription medicines and providing advice to patients.

Pharmacologist

Pharmacologists study the effects of drugs and chemicals on living things, and develop new products to help tackle disease.

Phlebotomist

Phlebotomists collect blood samples from patients, and send them off for analysis and testing

Physician Associate (PA):

While not brand new, this role is expanding rapidly to address doctor shortages. PAs are trained to perform duties like taking medical histories, conducting physical examinations, diagnosing illnesses, and managing treatment plans, all under the supervision of a doctor.

Physiotherapist

Helps people affected by injury, illness, or disability through movement and exercise, manual therapy, and education.

Physicist

Physicists study the behaviours of matter and energy and form theories to explain how everything fits together

Physiotherapist

Physiotherapists assess and treat mobility problems in patients caused by illness, injury, ageing or disability.

Play Therapist

Uses play to help children understand and cope with difficult experiences and emotional distress.

Plastic surgeon

Plastic surgeons perform operations to restore someone's movement or appearance either for personal reasons or following an illness or injury.

Podiatrist

Podiatrists diagnose and treat foot and ankle problems to improve people's mobility and quality of life.

Podiatry assistant

Podiatry assistants provide foot treatments and nail care under the supervision of a podiatrist.

Podiatrist/Chiropodist

Diagnoses and treats problems of the feet and lower limbs.

Principal Social Worker

Principal Social Worker is a senior role, often responsible for leading social work practice within a local authority or organisation. They play a key role in strategic decision-making and ensure that social work practice aligns with national standards and regulations.

Public Health Policy Advisor

Research, develop, and analyse health policy to influence government and organisational strategy.

Public Health Practitioner:

Develop and manage public health programmes on the ground (e.g. obesity, smoking cessation) There are various practice areas in public health which include health promotion, health improvement, health policy and management among others. Masters in Public Health is a popular programme in UK.

Public Health Analyst/Intelligence

Conducts data analysis, epidemiology, interpreting health data to inform decisions and reports.

Public health informatics

The systematic application of data, technology, and information systems to public health practice and research

Psychiatrist

Psychiatrists are doctors who diagnose and treat patients with mental health problems.

Psychological wellbeing practitioner

Psychological wellbeing practitioners treat and support people with mental health problems.

Psychologist

Psychologists apply the scientific study of the mind and how it affects behaviour to help people deal with real life issues.

Psychotherapist

Psychotherapists use talking therapies to help people deal with emotional, behavioural and mental health issues.

Q

Quality Assurance/Improvement Lead

Works to monitor and improve the quality and safety of care services, ensuring they meet regulatory standards (e.g., CQC).

R

Radiologist

A medical doctor who specializes in diagnosing and treating conditions using medical imaging techniques such as x-rays, MRIs, and CT scans.

Radiographer:

Diagnostic Radiographer: Uses imaging technology like X-rays, MRI, and CT scans to diagnose injuries and diseases.

Therapeutic Radiographer: Plans and delivers radiotherapy treatment to patients with cancer.

Registered Manager

Key professional in a care organization responsible for ensuring high-quality, person-centered care. Their main duties include: Overseeing the level of care provided and managing operational matters and acting as a role model for staff and ensuring compliance with care standards.

Residential Manager

Key individual who among other duties: Ensuring the smooth operation of residential facilities, overseeing staff, managing budgets and ensuring that the living environment meets regulatory standards and the needs of residents

Residential Support Worker:

Works in a children's or adult care home, providing 24-hour support and creating a safe, supportive environment.

Respiratory Physiologist:

Performs tests on patients' lungs to help diagnose and monitor respiratory conditions like asthma or COPD.

S

Social Prescribing Link Worker:

A key role in the NHS Long Term Plan. They connect patients with non-medical sources of support within the community (e.g., gardening groups, debt advice, art classes, walking clubs) to address the social determinants of health (loneliness, financial stress, housing).

Social Worker:

Works to protect vulnerable people from harm and support them to live independently. They work with children, families, adults, and the elderly.

Social Work Assistant

Social Work Assistants support qualified social workers by carrying out administrative tasks, supporting clients, and assisting with the implementation of care plans. This role is often a stepping stone for those who wish to become qualified social workers.

Social Work Consultant

Social Work Consultants provide expert advice, training, and support to social work teams and organisations. They are often brought in to lead on specific projects, improve practice, or address complex issues within services.

Social Work Manager

Social work managers oversee teams of social workers and ensure the delivery of high-quality services. They are responsible for the management and allocation of resources, staff supervision, and ensuring compliance with legal and regulatory standards.

Routes to Social Work Training in UK
https://www.prospects.ac.uk/job-profiles/social-worker

Sonographer

Sonographers use ultrasound equipment to screen and diagnose medical conditions.

Speech and Language Therapist

Speech and language therapy assistants support people who have difficulties with communication, or with eating, drinking or swallowing.

Speech and Language Therapist (SLT)

Assesses and treats speech, language, and communication problems in people of all ages, helping them to communicate to the best of their ability.

Substance Misuse Worker

Supports individuals who are addicted to drugs or alcohol, providing counselling, harm reduction advice, and pathways to recovery.

T

Telecare Coordinator

Manages the installation and monitoring of technology (e.g., personal alarms, sensors) that helps people, particularly the elderly, live safely at home.

Therapeutic Care Worker

Works with children and young people in care, using a therapeutic approach to help them recover from trauma and build healthy relationships.

U

Ultra sonographer/Sonographer

A specialist healthcare professional who uses ultrasound equipment to create images (sonograms) of internal body structures to aid diagnosis.

V

Volunteer Coordinator

Manages and supports the team of volunteers who provide essential non-clinical support across health and social care organisations.

Volunteer (Various)

Roles can include: hospital meet-and-greet, charity shop work, community transport driver, bereavement support, fundraising, and many more. A fantastic way to gain experience.

W

Welfare Rights Officer

Provides advice and advocacy to help people access the welfare benefits and financial support they are entitled to.

Wheelchair Services Engineer

Assesses patients' needs and provides, maintains, and repairs wheelchairs and other mobility equipment.

Wellbeing Manager / Workplace Health Consultant:

They work with companies and organisations to develop and implement strategies to support employee mental and physical health, reducing burnout and improving productivity. This is a growing field within corporate health.

X

X-ray Helper/Assistant

Supports the Radiographer in preparing patients and equipment for X-ray procedures. (Note: This is one of the few roles where the letter 'X' is directly applicable!).

Y

Youth Worker (in Health/Social Care)

Often works in community or charity settings to support the mental, emotional, and physical wellbeing of young people, providing a trusted point of contact.

Z

Zero-Hours Contract Worker:

While not a specific job title, this is a common type of contract in the social care sector (e.g., for Care Assistants and Support Workers). It offers flexibility but often less job security. Understanding contract types is an important part of a career in this sector.

CHAPTER 3

With a qualification in health and social care such as certificate, diploma and degree you can work in many different settings across the UK and beyond. Below are details of prospective employers in the health and social care sector.

National Health Service (NHS)

NHS is the largest employer in the UK and a leading recruiter of diploma holders. Its size means there are opportunities in almost every part of the country.

Typical roles: Healthcare Assistant, Support Worker, Nursing Associate.

Why work here: You get access to nationwide job opportunities, strong job security, and structured career progression. The NHS also offers good benefits, such as pensions, paid leave, and funded training.

Local Councils & Social Services

Local councils play a big role in adult social care and community services. They hire Health and Social care graduates to support individuals and families directly in the community.

Typical roles: Adult Social Care Worker, Child Support Worker, Community Outreach Worker.

Private Care Homes & Residential Facilities

Private care providers run care homes, nursing homes, and residential support services for older adults and people with complex needs.

Charities & Non-Profit Organisations

Charities are mission-driven employers focused on improving lives through targeted support. They work with vulnerable groups and often provide specialised services.

Private Healthcare Providers

Private healthcare companies offer clinical and non-clinical roles in hospitals, rehabilitation centres, and home care services.

Other Employers

There are many other employers who hire Health and Social Care graduates apart from the above mentioned.

CHAPTER 4

KEY THINGS TO KNOW ABOUT WORKING IN UK HEALTH AND SOCIAL CARE SECTOR

The NHS:

The National Health Service is the UK's publicly funded healthcare system and the largest employer in Europe. It is built on the principles of being free at the point of use for all UK residents. It is arguably the biggest employer in this sector mostly for health workers although there are opportunities also for social care workers.

Social Care:

This is care provided to vulnerable people (often the elderly or those with disabilities) in their own homes or in care homes. It is provided by local authorities, private companies, and charities. It is often means-tested (not free for everyone).

BASW Support

The British Association of Social Workers (BASW) is the professional association for social work and social workers in the United Kingdom (UK). The Code of Ethics states the values and ethical principles on which the profession is based.

CHAPTER 5

HEALTH AND SOCIAL CARE INSTITUTIONS IN UK

There are scores of universities and colleges that offer courses in health and social care in the United Kingdom from Level 3 to level 7 (Foundation to Masters).

https://collegedunia.com/uk/sciences/health-and-social-care-universities

Routes for Health and Social Care in UK: There are many pathways, including:

University Degrees: e.g., Nursing, Public Health, Medicine, Physiotherapy, Social Work.

Apprenticeships: A hugely popular route, allowing you to earn while you learn. Options range from Healthcare Support Worker to Nurse and Degree-level apprenticeships.

College Courses: e.g., T-Levels, BTECs, and NVQs in Health and Social Care.

Starting as an HCA/Support Worker: A common way to get experience and then train for a more senior role.

Health and Social Care Regulators in United Kingdom

General Chiropractic Council (GCC): www.gcc-uk.org

General Dental Council (GDC): www.gdc-uk.org

General Medical Council (GMC) www.gmc-uk.org

General Optical Council (GOC) www.goc-uk.org

General Osteopathic Council (GOsC): www.osteopathy.org.uk

General Pharmaceutical Council (GPhC): https://www.pharmacyregulation.org

Health Care Professions Council (HCPC) https://www.hcpc-uk.org.uk

Nursing and Midwifery Council (NMC): www.nmc-uk.org

Pharmaceutical Society of Northern Ireland (PSNI) https://psni.org.uk

Professional Standards Authority (PSA): https://www.professionalstandards.org.uk

Social Care regulators

Social Work England (SWE): https://www.socialworkengland.org.uk

Northern Ireland Social Care Council (NISCC): https://portal.niscc.org

Social Care Wales: https://socialcare.wales/

Scottish Social Services Council (SSSC): https://www.sssc.uk.com

CHAPTER 6

CONCLUSION

Health and social care is a huge industry in the United Kingdom and offers a diverse range of rewarding careers, each with its own peculiar responsibilities and requirements. Whether you aspire to care for patients directly, indirectly, working behind the scenes in healthcare administration, or specialise in a specific area of healthcare. It also offers huge opportunities for all those who are seeking a career in this huge and dynamic sector. Health and social care sector is one of the most state supported areas and is easily accessible to all qualified candidates across the United Kingdom. The aging population of the UK necessitates the need for the state support in the sector by way of huge financial investments. There is growing interest in joining this rewarding sector which is one of most diverse sectors in the UK. A career in Health and social care is essentially a straight route to employment for people of all backgrounds in UK. It is also one of the fastest growing areas of employment for graduates of all ages at all levels. This handbook will help you choose a suitable career among the many careers showcased.

REFERENCES

Andalo, Debbie (5 March 2019). "The NHS apprenticeships offering a new route to health and social care". The Guardian. Retrieved 28 September 2025.

BASW : https://new.basw.co.uk

Community Care: https://jobs.communitycare.co.uk/

Health and Social Care Diploma in UK :

https://uk.hfonline.org/course/health-and-social-care-diploma-2/?msclkid=0a8f89ab816c135da03ae0bc3b554311&utm_source=bing&utm_medium=cpc&utm_campaign=Sales%20-%20Search%20-%20Dynamic%20-%20Health%20%26%20Social%20Care&utm_term=Health%20and%20Social%20Care%20Diploma&utm_content=Health%20and%20Social%20Care%20Diploma

National Careers Service: https://nationalcareers.service.gov.uk/

NHS official website: https://www.england.nhs.uk/homepage

Nursing: https://www.gov.uk/government/collections/careers-in-nursing?

Prospects: https://www.prospects.ac.uk/job-profiles/social-worker
https://www.prospects.ac.uk/careers-advice/what-can-i-do-with-my-degree/health-studies

Skills for Care: https://www.skillsforcare.org.uk/

What is health and social care: https://www.twclondon.org.uk/blogs/what-is-health-and-social-care

Where to Study Social Work in UK: https://edurank.org/psychology/social-work/gb/#google_vignette

https://www.jobsmedical.co.uk

https://www.livecareer.co.uk

https://www.healthcareers.nhs.uk/explore-roles

https://www.cv-library.co.uk/Social-Care-jobs

https://www.reed.co.uk/jobs/health-care-jobs

https://jobs.theguardian.com/jobs/health

Nursing Jobs & Healthcare Careers

https://jobs.communitycare.co.uk/

https://www.british-nursingjobs.co.uk/

https://www.prospects.ac.uk/jobs-and-work-experience/job-sectors/healthcare

https://www.jobs.nhs.uk

https://carejobs.org.uk

www.ingramcontent.com/pod-product-compliance
Lightning Source LLC
Chambersburg PA
CBHW070942160426
43193CB00011B/1785